LOVE OUT LOUD

A book about Love, Life and Leadership

Now eagerly desire the greater gifts. And yet I will show you the most excellent way.
(1 Corinthians 12:31 NIV)

By
Emilio De La Cruz

Foreword By
Rev. Wilfredo (Choco) De Jesus

GATEWAY PRESS

**A Division of Aion Group Multimedia
and Gateway International Bible Institute**

Published by:

GATEWAY PRESS
A Division of Aion Group Multimedia
and Gateway International Bible Institute

20118 N 67th Ave
Suite 300-446
Glendale, Arizona 85308
www.aionmultimedia.com

Printed in the United States of America

ISBN:978-0991565719

FOREWORD

In Love out Loud, Pastor Emilio De La Cruz passionately shares his personal testimony on how his life was changed as he learned the transformative power of God's love for us. He learned the love described in John 3:16, "For God so loved the world that he gave his one and only Son, that whoever believes in him shall not perish, but have eternal life."

At the tender age of 18, De La Cruz found himself in prison serving time as an adult. He was filled with anger, rage; he felt hopeless and empty. Although he read the Bible in jail and made promises to the Lord that he would change, he wasn't really ready to change. Upon being released he continued his rebellious lifestyle. He persisted to smoke, drink and party until one day his girlfriend invited him to church (he even smoked a joint before going in) not taking church seriously.

De La Cruz didn't remember the sermon or the worship song, but he did remember he "felt something strange." That "strange" feeling had him return to the church, but this time sober. On this second occasion he remembers praying for God to remove his heart of stone and to give him a new heart. He accepted Jesus Christ as his Lord and Savior and quit smoking, drinking and partying that very instant. Since that moment, De La Cruz felt the indescribable love of Christ and has made it his call to show others that same unconditional love. As a Pastor, I'm still amazed at how God turns around our rebellious spirits, our struggles, pain, anger and hurt into something good. I love to witness that transformation when individuals whole-heartedly surrender their lives to Christ.

After 39 years serving the Lord, Pastor De La Cruz shares his lessons and calling in Love out Loud. God wants to use your pain in life to help others, but you've got to be open to forgiveness, love and peace that could only come when you surrender your heart to Christ. God became

i

one of us and lived among us in order to lead us out of darkness and into a marvelous light. Jesus is the best example of Love out Loud. How much does God love you? Jesus died on the cross for you, so that you may have eternal life – that is the greatest love of all.

Through the power of the Holy Spirit we activate God's desire for us to love others as we love ourselves. If you don't love yourself or you feel you are not worthy of being loved, I pray as your read the pages of this book, your Spirit is moved to understand that we were all created in God's image to do two things on Earth: learn to love God and learn to love other people. Life is all about love.

"And so we know and rely on the love God has for us. God is love. Whoever lives in love lives in God, and God in them." –
1 John 4:16

As you read this inspiring book by my good friend Pastor De La Cruz, may you experience the love of Christ in a new way as you learn to "Love out Loud."

God Bless you!

Wilfredo De Jesús
Senior Pastor, New Life Covenant Church, Chicago, IL

Table of Contents

Chapter 1:
Experiencing His Indescribable Love

My first encounter with His love was like an earthquake in my spirit; it shook me! It shook my universe.

God's love for me is so awesome, I can't begin to describe the greatness and beauty of His love. When I was lost, rebellious and vile, He loved me! He loved me enough to seek me out and find me; to persuade and convince me to trust Him. How could He love me the way I was? How could He give his life for a person with so much sin? I will never understand, but He did love me! He gave his life for me! I know I'm not the only one that He loves, but He makes me feel like I am! His love for me... When I experienced it for the first time, it stimulated every fiber of my being; it made me feel alive. His love for me... where else could I find anything like this? It resonated to the deepest parts of my soul. His love changed me in a way like nothing else could and He loved me so unreservedly, so completely and unconditionally. My first encounter with His love was like an earthquake in my spirit; it shook me! It shook my universe. God's love for me is so steadfast. Walking with him over the past 39 years, I have failed Him so many times- even though I am not given over to a sinful lifestyle, I remain sinful, undone, and highly imperfect yet He still loves me! It is this same love that has sustained me over the years. I would have given up so many times if not for a deep awareness of His love for me, for His great love manifested to me through His faithfulness, His mercy and His grace. Just knowing that He loves me is enough! I have never doubted His love; He has never allowed me to, never given me reason to. I love Him, too! I try to show my love in every way possible. I continually seek Him and surrender my will to Him; I stay grateful for all He does for me and I tell Him often that I love Him. I try with all my might to walk in obedience to Him and to keep sin out of my life. Sometimes, I wonder if He doubts my love for Him, but He knows my heart and He sees my works. I don't want Him to ever doubt my love for Him. I believe that if he ever stopped loving me (which I believe is impossible), I would stop existing. I need Him to love me and I need to be reassured of His love for me. Sometimes, I still can't believe it! Sometimes I still can't believe that the God of the universe would love me so much.

At the age of 18, my life was a mess. My dad left us when I was eight-years-old, and my mom would bring men into the house. We always lived in an environment of violence and alcoholism. I grew up with a lot of anger and became violent. I was in and out of jail, constantly using drugs and alcohol, involved in many fights and even came to a place where I was capable of killing someone. In my heart, I couldn't wait until the day I would have an opportunity to kill my dad because of the abandonment and rejection that I felt. The rage in me was deep. When I would fight, I was capable of murder. Sometimes I would try to gouge out eyes, and I almost always carried a knife- and was capable of using it. My life was so miserable; I was dead inside and I felt empty and alone. I was involved in robberies, a high-speed chase with the police, fights, and a riot in my high school. At least one time I seriously contemplated committing a murder. On one occasion someone held a gun to my head; instantly I began to contemplate how I would kill this person. I was arrested on several occasions; one time the officer told me afterward that if I had moved he would have shot me. I had been reported as being armed and dangerous. At the age of 18, I was in a jail- ready to be tried as an adult and facing prison time.

God came on strong. My sister had been saved and she would park outside the jail house to pray for me during her lunch hour. On my birthday, April 17th, 1975, I received two gifts while I was in jail; a book called "How to Stop Worrying and Start Living" and a Bible. One of the men with me in jail was going to prison for life. He warned me not to read the Bible. He said that he had an aunt who started reading the Bible and she went crazy. I started reading it anyway. Though I remember finding comfort in what I read, I honestly can't say that anything jumped out of the pages and spoke to me. What I do remember is that one day I got a feeling inside of me, and I thought to myself, "There has to be more to life than this." Somehow I was released from jail and put on probation. Though I had made some promises to God while in jail like, "I will only drink at home" and "I will only use alcohol and marijuana", none of that was remembered as soon as I was free. I continued living my "partying" lifestyle.

Not long after, I was invited to attend a church service by a girlfriend. Somehow I convinced about five of my friends to join me, and we went to church. We smoked a few joints of marijuana before going in and entered an Assembly of God Church for the first time. The church was packed. There were around two-hundred people there. We were escorted to the only empty bench, in the very front. The music started to play, and the people started to sing. Everyone was singing with so much energy. I don't remember the sermon that was preached.

When we left the church and got in our car, we all agreed that we had felt something strange. I didn't understand any of it; I didn't pray a prayer, I didn't find faith, I did not make a commitment to Christ, I just attended church and "felt something strange". But from that night on, I lost every desire to smoke marijuana or drink alcohol. I kept going to the parties, but I would fake it; dumping out my beer when no one was watching and acting like I was smoking the marijuana. I was not the same, and I really didn't even know why. All I knew was that I felt drawn back to church.

Some weeks later, I returned to the church; this time alone. I sat in the very back and again the music and the singing was vibrant; people were excited. The preacher preached, and again, I don't really remember what he preached. When he made a call for people to come forward to receive Christ, I was glued to my seat. Then he said, "If you want to receive Christ, you can kneel right where you are and ask him into your heart." I knelt there in the very back of the church and when I knelt some words that the preacher had said came to my mind: "I will remove the heart of stone and replace it with a heart of flesh". I asked God to do that for me; to remove my hard heart of stone and give me a new heart. At that moment, I felt the love of God come all over me. When I met Jesus, His great love transformed me into a new creation. Love began to overflow from my new heart. I loved my dad, and even those who had abused me. When I look back at my old life, at my old self, I hardly believe it myself. He loved me then, and I love Him now. For all my days, I will love Him.

I know that He loves me, but what is unfathomable is that He loves me with all of His heart. He does! He loves me with all of His heart! Even though He makes me feel like I'm the only one He loves this way, I know that His love is infinite. He loves you just as much as He loves me. I believe that love (God's love) does make the world go around. I believe that what the world needs now is love, sweet love. Not just any love; it has to be God's

4

love. I do believe that the world will be a better place if we can just "put a little love in your heart", but it has to be God's love!

"What's love got to do with it?" EVERYTHING! God's love is the answer, the antidote and the greatest power in the universe. As I write about "love" I will be writing about God's love; nothing fake, nothing fabricated and nothing human. God's love manifests in our humanity. God's love (agape) is allowed to flow in our everyday lives. He commands us to walk in His love and to grow in love. I'm believing that this book will help you in your journey of walking, living and leading with love. This book will have many scriptures from the Bible, and I encourage you to meditate on these scriptures. Let them go deep into your heart. Ask God to make them real to you. The following scripture tells us that we can "know the love of Christ, which passes knowledge". To know His love, we have to understand it with a knowledge beyond human knowledge; it will only be by the Spirit of God that we will be able to gain this understanding. But it is only by knowing the love of Christ that we can be "filled with all the fulness of Christ"

Ephesians 3:14-19
"For this reason I bow my knees to the Father of our Lord Jesus Christ, from whom the whole family in heaven and earth is named, that He would grant you, according to the riches of His glory, to be strengthened with might through His Spirit in the inner man, that Christ may dwell in your hearts through faith; that you, being rooted and grounded in love, may be able to comprehend with all the saints what is the width and length and depth and height— to know the love of Christ which passes knowledge; that you may be filled with all the fullness of God."

LOVE OUT LOUD

This must be our prayer for our own lives, for our loved ones and the people that God has given us to oversee; that they might be rooted and grounded in love and know the love of Christ.

Perhaps the greatest evangelist from the past is Dwight L. Moody. Dwight L. Moody was born in 1837, and he was born again in 1854 at the age of seventeen through the instrumentality of a man named Edward Kimball. He was in business until age twenty-three, and he entered the ministry as a lay preacher. He was not well educated, yet he established schools that still stand to this day. He was successful, to a point, in his early years of ministry that began about 1860. As you can well imagine, from reading the date, you know the turbulent times that were going on in America. This was during the Civil War. Moody made a missions trip in 1867 to England when he was thirty-seven years old. He met a man named Henry Morehouse. Morehouse wanted to preach for Moody, but Moody kept putting him off. One day, Morehouse invited himself saying that he was going to be in Chicago. He came, and the year was 1867. He preached on John 3:16 while Moody was gone. "For God so loved the world that He gave His only begotten Son that whoever believes in Him should not perish but have everlasting life."

Moody came back from a trip and asked what Morehouse was preaching about. The congregants said, "John 3:16." Moody thought it was rather elementary, and he said, "Well what is he going to preach on next?"
They said, "John 3:16."
He asked, "Well, is it a two-part message?"
They said, "No. He said he is going to preach on John 3:16 until we learn it."

EXPERIENCING HIS INDESCRIBABLE LOVE

Morehouse continued for weeks on John 3:16. The following are the words of Dwight L. Moody, who sat there and listened to this man who preached on John 3:16...

> "I never knew, up to that time, that God loved me so much. This heart of mine began to thaw out. I could not keep back the tears. I just drank it in. I tell you, there is one thing that draws above everything else in the world and that is love. I took up that word "love", and I do not know how many weeks I spent in studying the passages in which it occurs, till at last I could not help loving people. I had been feeding on love so long that I was anxious to do good for everybody I came in contact with. I got full of it. It ran out my fingers. You take up the subject of love in the Bible, you will get so full of it that all you have to do is open your lips and a flood of the love of God flows out. The churches would soon be filled if outsiders could find that people in them loved them when they came. This love draws sinners. We must win them to us first. Then we can win them to Christ. We must get people to love us, and then turn them over to Christ. If you haven't got love in your heart, you should throw your hope to the four winds and go and get a better one. There is nothing greater than the love of God."

"Do you know that nothing you do in this life will ever matter, unless it is about loving God and loving the people he has made?"
— Francis Chan, Crazy Love: Overwhelmed by a Relentless God

Chapter 2:
Learning To Love

From the day I met and fell in love with Jesus, all anger and bitterness left me. From the beginning, my walk was a walk with Him; everything else was secondary, every other relationship was secondary. I could not and would not let anything damage this new relationship that I had with the King of Glory. I found it easy to love others- even those who offended me. God wants us to love one another because this is what will really make us happy. God wants us to love one another because this is the only way that we will ever complete His work. We were made to operate in perfect unity. To do so, we have to operate in perfect love. From the day I came to Christ, I do not remember not loving someone. That's the kind of work God did in my life. Yet, I'm still learning how to love the way that He loves; I'm still growing in His infinite love.

If we are to "know the love of Christ which surpasses all knowledge", we have to be willing to learn. Not just Bible memorization, not even mere illumination, but we have to come to the acknowledgment that we have only scratched the surface, that indeed we know so little. Love is not an accomplishment. It's not as if one day you just get it, and then you have it for the rest of your life. Love is the fruit of walking with God daily and allowing

His Holy Spirit to control your mind, your emotions, your words, your heart and soul.

Love is like a tree that grows within you; it starts as a seed- the seed of Gods love- it takes root, and then it grows and grows and grows. There are no limits to how great this love can grow other than limits we place there ourselves. For a love to grow great, it has to have deep roots and a strong foundation. It is only to the measure that it reflects in our own lives that we have known His love. It's amazing to look at scripture and see that it never records that Jesus ever said, "I love you" to anyone, and yet, His life and His actions manifested a love that permeated to everyone around Him.

Most of us have learned a very superficial love. Some had the privilege of being raised by a godly parent who consistently reflected God's love- while others had ungodly parents who were abusive, cruel, harsh and self-serving. Many of us have had to learn love from ground zero; struggling with the false perceptions, impressions and concepts of love that were branded into our hearts. This is why God pours His love into our hearts. As it is written in Romans chapter 5, "And this hope will not lead to disappointment. For we know how dearly God loves us, because he has given us the Holy Spirit to fill our hearts with his love." That's what starts us out in this great journey- His love poured into us, a new experience of a new love. A love that we had never known before- or at the most, we have only seen glimpses of His love. But now God pours it into us; He fills our hearts with His love.

Now we can grow in His love, now we do not just have knowledge of His love, but now we have personally experienced His love in our most inner being (Ephesians 3:17). Paul prays for God's people to be rooted in this love. Let it become our source of life. Just like a root drinks up the water of life, we must drink up continually of God's love. His love is our life source. Without continually drinking of His love, we will dry up and die. We have to continually- daily- think about His love for us. We must constantly meditate on the richness of His love toward us.

It is so easy for us to get caught up trying to prove our love for Him, trying to please Him and to serve Him, that we, like Martha, forget to sit at His feet and soak in His wonderful love for us. Paul also prays for the Ephesians to be "grounded in love". Here, he uses the two metaphors of agriculture and of construction. To me, it is important that *rooted* comes first, and then *grounded*. Our works have to flow from our relationship. Faith must work by love. To be rooted in love is to sit at his feet, the better part, the necessity. To be grounded in love is to labor with Him and for Him. He said, "If you love me, obey." Just as we grow in our obedience to God, we must grow in love.

One thing that is essential for us to grow in our love for God is to love God's children.

1 John 4:7-8
"Beloved, let us love one another: for love is of God; and every one that loveth is born of God, and knoweth God. He that loveth not knoweth not God; for God is love."

God places great importance on us loving one another. Jesus called this a new commandment. How do we know if we are showing love to one another? If we love each other, we do not speak evil of each other. Out of love, we will speak only words that build up and not tear down. We help each other in times of need. We prefer one another. The church – called out ones, the body of Christ – members one with the other (the family of God) and are joined together through an agape (Greek word for the love of God) relationship. Loving each other the way that God wants us to, will require that we keep ourselves filled with His love.

This is why worship and being in His presence- spending time with him, walking with Him- is so vital. Love has to flow from Him to us, so that it can flow through us, to others. The flesh does not know how to love; not with agape love. All other love is selfish at the core; love with a payoff, love that "makes me feel good." Only agape love is selfless. We need the love of God. The Bible says that He poured His love on our hearts by His Spirit.

When we were born again, our hearts received an overflowing of God's love (you remember)! You just walked around loving everyone. For some, it did not last very long because they put their eyes on the imperfections and failures of others and they lost the love. But if you had a personal encounter with Christ, you had this love at least for a while. Some new Christians become disillusioned and discouraged right away, but this is where we have to learn to love God and love others through His love-unconditional love.

Consider the kind of unity Jesus prayed for in John 17:11 "Now I am no longer in the world, but these are in the world, and I come to You. Holy Father, keep through Your name those whom You have given Me, that they may be one as we are."

The fruit of the Spirit is love, and the priority of love is unity in the family of God. This is why the enemy fights so hard to bring disunity, dissension and division in the church. The devil's toolbox is called "the flesh". The enemy uses anger as a hammer to bring pain and destruction. He uses control like pliers gripping hearts and minds; the annoying behaviors - such as nagging, ignoring, arrogance - are like sandpaper in the enemy's hands.

Ephesians 4:3 AMP
"Be eager and strive earnestly to guard and keep the harmony and oneness that is of [and is produced by] the Spirit in the binding power of peace."

It's His unity- it's important to Him- it's the priority of His fruit. Unity in our marriage, unity in our home, unity in our church; unity brings peace, and peace is prosperity!

The Prayer of Jesus

John 17:20-21 NKJV
"I do not pray for these alone, but also for those who will believe in Me through their word; vs. 21 that they all may be one, as You, Father, are in Me, and I in You; that they also may be one in Us, that the world may believe that You sent Me."

Jesus was praying for you and me- for us to have unity as the unity between Him and His Father (a perfect unity), and it will only be perfected through Gods love! When we have this unity, the unity of the body will release faith in a lost world to believe that Jesus is Lord. Revival depends on the unity of Gods people.

John 17:22 NKJV
"And the glory which You gave me I have given them, that they may be one just as we are one."

We have His glory (goodness) to help us be one. Heavenly goodness is in us if we let it flow. His love is his goodness that can flow through us, and *must* flow through us if we are going to come into PERFECT unity.

LOVE OUT LOUD

Verse 23, *"I in them, and You in me; that they may be made perfect in one, and that the world may know that You have sent me, and have loved them as You have loved me."*

Us loving one another is proof of God's love.
If the world sees us loving one another, it will believe God loves them and that He sent Jesus to die for them.

1 Peter 4:8 (NKJV)
"And above all things have fervent love for one another, for love will cover a multitude of sins."

Love brings us into unity with imperfect people. Love will equip us to accomplish God's eternal purposes. There are things that we can only accomplish together. We need His love to have unity to accomplish His will.

Come Holy Spirit; fill us with His love again!

The unity that only comes through the Spirit is not of the flesh. It only comes if we genuinely love one another. Being in love with God and being in love with God's word are validated by being in love with God's family. Loving the family of God is the fruit of loving God and His word. God is our father and His command is for us to love one another. The Bible is filled with instructions on how to love one another.

Romans 5:5 NKJV
"Now hope does not disappoint, because the love of God has been poured out in our hearts by the Holy Spirit who was given to us."

If you are a born again child of God, then the Holy Spirit has poured God's love into your heart. You have no excuse not to love; God's love is not just put in your heart, but *poured* in. Your heart has been filled to overflowing with God's love; you just have to let it flow!

John 15:10 NKJV
"If you keep my commandments you will abide in my love, just as I have kept my fathers commandments and abide in His love."

Love is not just an emotion. I do not think you have love without emotion; real love has a powerful, passionate emotion that is not always on the surface, but it is always there deep inside. Love is walking in submission to God, and loving one another is walking in submission to each other. God's commandments are not just to show us that He is in charge; His commands are all for our good and given to us out of His great love for us. So that out of our love for Him- out of our relationship with him and our trust toward Him as our loving father- we keep His commands. You cannot say that you love God and not trust Him! To trust Him is to love Him. Men sometimes cannot be trusted, but God is worthy of all of our trust; all of the time. God is trustworthy. If you love God, you will trust Him.

John 17:26 CEB
"I've made your name known to them and will continue to make it known so that your love for me will be in them, and I myself will be in them."

The purpose of revealing the Father to us was to reveal the father's love, so that His love could be in us- which is Christ in us! You see, this whole concept of Christ in us, "the indwelling of the Holy Spirit", "Jesus in my heart" thing, all has to do with love. Agape has to be in us for Christ to dwell in us. If Christ is in us, then God's love is in us.

LOVE OUT LOUD

Romans 12:10 NKJV
"Be kindly affectionate to one another with brotherly love, in honor giving preference to one another."

Love has to be lived out! The Bible says to love in deed and not just in word. In other words, *show me love.* Here it says, "Be kindly affectionate to one another with brotherly love..." I love to hug! I'm not saying you have to, but here it says to be affectionate. Greet one another with a holy kiss.

I remember a young man in Bible school; He was a rough guy who came through teen challenge. He would say, "I don't believe in all that hugging stuff; that's sissy." Then one day he was baptized in the Holy Spirit, and when he got up from the altar, guess what he did? You got it! He started hugging everyone! It may not come easy to you, but show some affection; show the love.

1 Peter 1:22 NKJV
"Since you have purified your souls in obeying the truth through the Spirit in sincere love of the brethren, love one another fervently with a pure heart."

Loving one another is the Spirit helping us to obey the truth. The truth is that God commands us expressively to love one another. Not just that- but He commands us to love one another *fervently*. The dictionary defines *fervently* as "marked by great intensity of feeling." Strong's Concordance gives us the Greek word for *fervently*; ektenos - "properly, fully stretched, i.e. describing the verbal idea as extended out, to its necessary (full) potential ("without slack"); strenuously, without undue let up." That's the way God tells us to love each other; that's loving out loud! As the family of God, we go through so much together. Sometimes our own will do things (or say things) that hurt us deeply. We cannot stop loving; we cannot allow bitterness to come into our hearts. We must forgive and come back to the first love. It does not mean that the relationship can always be brought back to what it was, but the love can be restored.

1 John 1:7 AMP
"But if we [really] are living and walking in the light, as He [Himself] is in the light, we have [true, unbroken] fellowship with one another, and the blood of Jesus Christ His Son cleanses (removes) us from all sin and guilt [keeps us cleansed from sin in all its forms and manifestations]."

I know this verse does not say "love", but it's there. Where? "...we have true, unbroken fellowship with one another..." That takes love; that takes commitment.

One of the biggest mistakes made by believers today is to underestimate the value of church attendance and involvement. The church has been attacked through the centuries by the devil, by the world and even by Christians themselves. Many times, you will hear Christians and even preachers criticize "the church". In criticizing the church, we criticize ourselves; for we are the church. Jesus said the gates of hell will not prevail against the church, and the church- the fellowship of the redeemed- has withstood against every assail and onslaught of the enemy. To think that you can be strong, fruitful and faithful without commitment, service, attendance and involvement in the local church, is to go against all that the scriptures declare. Attend your church at least twice a week; be involved, become a "minister" in your church, use your gifts to build up the body of Christ.

Christianity without church attendance is like starving to death with a kitchen full of food. Putting God first includes a commitment to be an active member of a local church.

LOVE OUT LOUD

How can Christians not attend church regularly?
How can one love God, and not love God's children?

A person who does not attend church because of people's faults says that he is better than everyone else. We are called to be part of a fellowship of believers and to walk together in love with a church family. The verse goes on to say something that to me is a little mysterious (Ok, maybe not to you but to me- I'm not a great theologian). It says, "...if we walk in the light we have fellowship with one another..." Now whenever I see the word *if*, I always ask myself if the opposite is true. If we have fellowship, the blood of Christ cleanses us from all sin. So, if we do not have fellowship, does the opposite hold true? It stands to reason, or at least that's the way I see it.

Fellowship is not optional; it is vital! The absence of fellowship is the absence of love. If you are not a committed part of a church family, you are not walking in love, and you are missing out on some of the great life-giving benefits of the sacrifice of Jesus Christ. I cannot say, "I love you, but I just don't want to spend any time with you." You cannot fulfill all of God's commands concerning love and not be a part of a fellowship of believers. D.L. Moody said, "Church attendance is as vital to a disciple as a transfusion of rich, healthy blood to a sick man."

Love is of God

LEARNING TO LOVE

Agape love comes from God! The absence of God is the absence of love, and the absence of love is the absence of God. Any capacity in us to show real love comes from God. The Bible says that, in the last days, the love of many shall wax cold. This is because men will turn away from God. We see it today in our own nation. People are not just atheist; they are anti-Christ; thus the absence of love.

The more love you give, the more you have. Love is the one treasure that multiplies by division. The more you take away from it and give it away, the more it increases. You can give it all away today, and tomorrow morning you will have more. If you hold back your love, it begins to grow cold and hard.

In Israel, there are two seas; the sea of Galilee and the Dead Sea. Water flows into and out of the sea of Galilee. The sea of Galilee is alive and full of life. The Dead Sea is another story; it gives nothing out. Everything that comes in stays there, and thus it's the "Dead" Sea. This is how love operates in our lives. As long as it keeps flowing in and flowing out, our lives will be fruitful and life-giving. But if the flow stops, our spiritual lives will die.

God is the source of love. I need to be connected to Him so that His love can continue to flow and increase in me. As we love God with all of our heart, mind and strength, our ability to love others increases.

Everyone who loves is born of God and knows God. People say they love, or say "I love you." Some say, "I love you" and are unfaithful. Some say, "I love you" and are abusive. Some stay with an abuser and say, "I love him." This is not loving. Someone cannot truly love you and abuse you. This is not loving; this is a lie. You cannot truly love someone who abuses you; what you feel is not love, not real love. This Bible verse is saying that

19

everyone who is born of God loves with God's love-unconditional, true love. This is saying that the true proof of being born of God is love!

God's love is greater than faith and greater than hope. Faith and hope are great for many things, but they do not build relationships. The fruit of the spirit (Galatians 5) is all about building relationships.

Galatians 5:22-23 CEB
"But the fruit of the Spirit is love, joy, peace, long-suffering, kindness, goodness, faithfulness, gentleness, and self-control. There is no law against things like this."

It does not say "...the fruits of the Spirit..." (plural), but "...the fruit of the Spirit..." (singular). I see it as a pomegranate; one fruit, but inside are the many little pieces. All of these together make up love. If one is missing, it's not complete.

I see the first two as pertaining to the love between you and God; to find joy in Him. Joy in His love for me - and in my love for Him and this relationship - results in peace between us and peace in my heart. The following five pertain to my relationship with others; long-suffering (or patience toward those I love), kindness, goodness, faithfulness and gentleness. All have to do with how I treat others. The last one I see as a perfecting of the others, a self-control so that I can more fully and more continually walk in the Spirit and continue to manifest His fruit.

The Spirit produces love; love produces joy; joy produces peace. From peace comes long-suffering (patience), from patience comes kindness, from kindness comes goodness; goodness produces faithfulness, faithfulness produces gentleness and from gentleness comes self-control.

If you do not have love, you do not have anything! Be sure to have love. Do not leave home without it (or get home without it). Love comes from God's Spirit. So if we have God's Spirit in us, then love should just naturally abound in us - right? Yet there are many Christians who lack love.

Galatians 5:17-18 NKJV
"For the flesh lusts against the Spirit, and the Spirit against the flesh; and these are contrary to one another, so that you do not do the things that you wish. But if you are led by the Spirit, you are not under the law."

The flesh fights the Spirit, and the main objective of the flesh is to "stop the love". The main objective of the Spirit is to produce "more love". Our part is not to give fruit (it's not our fruit), our part is to be in the spirit, yield to the spirit, live in the spirit and walk in the spirit. Three things are essential for us to do this:

No. 1 Dedication
A feeling of very strong support for, or loyalty to, someone or something : the quality or state of being dedicated to a person.

No. 2 Consecration
To make or declare sacred; especially : to devote irrevocably to the worship of God by a solemn ceremony; to devote to a purpose with or as if with deep solemnity or dedication

No. 3 Self-denial
A restraint or limitation of one's own desires or interests

LOVE OUT LOUD

It's going to take something on your part; you have to decide, you have to make a commitment to make some sacrifices. The Spirit is fighting for you, but the flesh is fighting against you, and the flesh is you. We need strength! There is strength in Christ. Love only comes from the Spirit. Only love can defeat the flesh. The Holy Spirit can only do His work of producing love when we abide (remain) in Christ and His word.

Your biggest problem is your flesh; only the spirit can defeat the flesh. The reason you cannot love enough to forgive - to be patient, not get angry, to love your enemies - is because the flesh gets in the way. Why do I need more love? My biggest problem is my flesh, and only love can defeat the flesh.

There are people who have great faith to believe for great things and do great things, but they cannot get along with anyone. The greatest way to get to know God is to let Him love through you in your family relationships.

1 John 4:8
"He that does not love does not know God."

If you do not love others, you do not know God! It's not just about loving God, but loving one another. We must learn how to love others! Again, it's not an obtained quality, but a learned characteristic.

Purpose! Practice! Persist!

Learning to love others will be a process. Learning to walk in love will be just like learning to walk. One step; then two, and then a lot of practice until you have perfected your walk. Love is thinking of someone before yourself. It means sharing your time and attention with someone, over-looking their shortcomings, encouraging them, and helping them when they're down.

You have to **purpose** in your heart first that you are going to love God and love others. It will have to be a daily decision; love must be intentional. This is how you begin to **practice** love. This means that the more you practice love, the better you become at it. What you are learning is how to let God's love flow through you. Finally, you must **persist**.

Agape love is not just the mushy, feel-good kind of love. Don't get me wrong, it does feel good to love, but sometimes it can be hard, and it can require great sacrifice. Many times, others will not reciprocate, and we might feel rejected. We will be tempted not to love, to take offense and become bitter. There will be times when it will require great work and great determination to continue to love.

Many times, the most difficult one to love is ourselves. We will fall short; we will fail, we will sin. When we came to Christ, we were so sure of our love for Him. We did love Him with all of our hearts but then came the temptation - the test of our love. We all failed the test in someway or another.

Peter said, "Lord I will die for you." Shortly thereafter he denied the Lord three times. Oh, the guilt and the shame he must have felt as he wept bitterly. We, too, know that guilt and that shame; we, too, have wept bitterly after having "denied" Him. But we can know that His love for us is unconditional, eternal, and unwavering. Because He still loves us, we can also learn to love ourselves.

LOVE OUT LOUD

LOVING YOURSELF

I'm not against all of the secular philosophies about self-love. Although I know that a lot of them are rooted in selfishness, pride and arrogance, I do believe that God wants us to have a good concept of ourselves and a godly self-image. God even says (Ephesians 5:29) "For no one ever hated his own flesh but nourishes and cherishes it"

"How can I love myself and know that I am not proud or selfish?" Love yourself with God's love. Love what God loves! If God loves you, you can love you with that same love. I believe that God wants us to love him first, love others second and love ourselves third. Only when we learn to love ourselves the way God does (unconditionally) can we truly begin to love others with that same love. It is also true that we will never love ourselves with a healthy, holy love until we love God with all of our hearts; for God is love!

Love is the essence of God; it is who God is. It's what God is all about. It is His very nature to love. What God loves most, is us! He has created us to pour His love on us, to make us the the object of His great love. God is love! He never stops loving us, even if we are rebellious, even if we are vile, even if we have fallen a million times, God is love.

Look at what love is, not just what love does. Love does what it does because love is what it is. Rather, love is who it is for, love is God (God is love) and if God dwells in you, then love dwells in you and to the degree that you love shows how much of God is in you!

Chapter 3:
The Agape Love Revolution

Do you want to start a revolution; one that can change your life, change your environment, change your marriage, change your children, your church, your community and the world?! God's love can do that. Not just by God loving the world, but us loving God and God's love flowing through us to love others. It can happen. It is happening here and there, but when we, God's people, fall in love with God, we will start a revolution like this world has never seen. I believe it's going to happen.

Luke 10:27
"So he answered and said, 'You shall love the Lord your God with all your heart, with all your soul, with all your strength, and with all your mind,' and 'your neighbor as yourself.'"

To truly love others, you must first love God with all your heart, mind, soul and strength. This was what Jesus called the first and greatest commandment. He said the second was to love your neighbor as yourself. If you love God, you will love yourself in the true sense, and then you will love others with the same love. The command God gives us is not just to love Him, but to be passionately in love with Him. This is why he said, "...with all your heart, soul, strength and mind..."

25

LOVE OUT LOUD

Loving God is not the same as being in love with God; the first denotes a mindset and a decision; the second a passionate relationship and a romance. We need both. The passionate love is what is missing in the lives of so many believers. So many love God intellectually, but not passionately. Some never even tell God that they love him anymore, and their rational is "I don't have to tell him, I just show him," - which reminds me of the wife that tells her husband, "You don't tell me that you love me anymore." To which the husband responds, "I told you twenty years ago when we were married. If I change my mind, I will let you know."

God loves when we tell him how much we love him; this is called praise! Just read the psalms; these were David's love letters to God. Do you write love letters to God? If you never have, you should try it. It worked for David. Here is one of my love letters to God:

> "You called me by my name, and you knew that I would fail again. You knew every sin, every dark thought, still you cheered me to the finish line. You knew that I would love you, through the storm and through the fire. You knew my love could not be stopped, not by foolish sin nor Satan's lies. This love of mine it can't be stopped, you loved me first and now I'm loving you back."

Falling in love with God will mark the beginning of a revolution in every area of your life.

revə-lo-oSHən
"a sudden, complete or marked change in something"

26

THE AGAPE LOVE REVOLUTION

"Falling in love with God..." You're probably thinking "I love God", but I'm not just asking if you love God. "Are you in love with God?" You can say "I love my life" or "I love my dog" or "I love pizza", but you never say, "I am *in love* with pizza" or "I'm *in love* with my dog"; at least I hope you never do. True love can only be found in a relationship with another person, and even then, so much of what is called "love" today is just lust.

So many are in love with money or pleasure, but it's not true love; it's carnal love; it's lust. So many get married because of passion, but many times the passion dies out, and they look for a new passion. In our Christian life, it's not enough to love "the things of God", love ministry, love worship, and love church. God demands to be your first love! Jesus asks Peter three times, "Do you love me?" Not, "Will you serve me?" or "Will you follow me?" He said, "Do you love me more than everything?" Peter responded, "I like you a lot." That's not enough!

He will keep asking you until you say it with passion, until you shout out "I LOVE YOU!" Jesus says in Matthew 22:37-40 that the greatest of all commandments is "Love the Lord your God WITH ALL your heart, mind, soul and strength." This is why Jesus tells the church (Revelation 2:1-4) of Ephesus, "I have something against you. You are a great church, you have great works, you have great discernment, you make great sacrifices, you are movers and shakers, but you don't have that red hot passionate love for me."

A person who is in love with God will be affected by this love in every area of his or her life. This love will produce a complete surrender, and the person in love with God will not be able to resist full obedience, unreserved service working for God, worshiping God and giving will flow from agape love. You are under the influence of agape love, intoxicated with your love for God. A person in love with God will feel like David when He said "as the deer pants for the water stream, so my heart pants for you, O God." 2 Corinthians 5:14 MSG says the love of God constrains us; "Christ's love has moved me to such extremes (to leave everything and to make sacrifices). His love has to be the first and last word in everything we do."

His love constrains us with irresistible power that limits us to the one great object- to the exclusion of other considerations. The Greek implies "to compress forcibly the energies into one channel." Love is jealous of any rival object engrossing the soul. This is a godly, righteous, holy jealousy that the Apostle Paul experienced for the church at Corinth when they were being moved away from their true love, Jesus (2 Co 11:1-3). "Oh that you would bear with me in a little folly - and indeed you do bear with me. For I am jealous for you with godly jealousy. For I betrothed you to one husband, than I may present you as a chaste virgin to Christ." God is a jealous God. Idolatry is to hunger for something, more that what you hunger for God. Idolatry is to love something more than you love God.

Love is powerful. It takes control of your life, and so God demands proof of our love for Him.

John 15:15
"If you love me, keep my commandments".

In Galatians 5:6 we read "Faith works by love..." Not by tradition or religion; not a force of habit or because of ambition. Faith works by love! The heroes of faith in Hebrews 11 were intoxicated with their love for God; the apostles were in love with God. Those today who leave all to serve Him who go to the jungles and the unreached parts of the earth, they do it constrained by love. What are you doing today because of the love God has given you, and because your heart is ablaze with a red hot passionate love for God?

At the age of eight-teen, I knew about Jesus from what I had been told by others- but I had never read a Bible or listened to someone preaching the gospel. I was living in the United States, but I was probably as ignorant as someone living in a nation where the gospel was not readily available. In short, I had grown up pretty much in a Godless environment. After attending church for the second time (out of great personal need), I gave my life to God, and asked Jesus Christ to be my savior and come into my life and my heart. I asked Him to give me a new heart and change my life. It was not my great knowledge of God's word that changed my life; it was not eloquent persuasion or emotional hype. What changed and revolutionized my life forever was that I fell in love with Jesus.

I fell madly in love with Him; He consumed my thoughts, my time, my dreams and my life- as He has done so to this day. There is nothing that I would not attempt to do for Him; there is nothing that I would not sacrifice because of His great love for me. I have seen people come to Christ out of need, seeking help, looking for deliverance and God faithfully hears their cry and delivers them from bondage. However, something is missing. They are like the nine lepers who go on their way. Though they might have been thankful for what they received, they never made the connection. They never realized that the reason that God came into their miserable lives was because He wanted to have a love relationship with them. Only one came back; only one fell at his feet; only one fell in love with him.

LOVE GIVES YOU POWER

LOVE OUT LOUD

The words to the old song *Love Will Keep Us Together* ring so truly to our relationship with God. Not primarily our love, but His love. It's His love first, and foremost, that is responsible for our perseverance. Romans 8:35-39 NKJV says, "Who shall separate us from the love of Christ? Shall tribulation, or distress, or persecution, or famine, or nakedness, or peril, or sword? As it is written: 'For Your sake we are killed all day long: We are accounted as sheep for the slaughter.' Yet in all these things we are more than conquerors through Him who LOVED us. For I am persuaded that neither death nor life, nor angels nor principalities nor powers, nor things present nor things to come, nor height nor depth, nor any other created thing, shall be able to separate us from the LOVE OF GOD which is in Christ Jesus our Lord."

Wow, wow, wow! Do you see it? It's His love that makes us more than conquerors and nothing, absolutely nothing, can take that love away from us!!! Yes, we love Him, yes we strive to please Him, yes we persevere and endure, but we could never do it without His love! We could never do any of it if He stopped loving us.

Do you want to start a revolution- a love revolution? That's what Jesus did. He loved his disciples and he loved the people. Even the Roman soldiers who crucified him, he loved them too, and prayed "Father, forgive them." Do you want to start a revolution? Do what Jesus says in Luke 6:1, "Love your enemies." Love those who mistreat you; those who overlook you, those who fail you and yes, those who cause you harm.

In verse 32 Jesus says, "But if you love those who love you, what credit is that to you? For even sinners do the same." Then, in verse 35 (yes it's there in the Bible; read it for yourself), "But love your enemies, do good, and lend, hoping for nothing in return; and your reward will be great, and you will be sons of the Most High."

Let's start a love revolution! This is one of the factors that propelled the Jesus movement of the 70's (I know, I was there). With all of our faults and hangups, we fell in love with Jesus and we would spread that love everywhere. We need another generation of love people. We need another generation that will fall madly, deeply, radically, head-over-heels in love with Jesus. We need a generation that will not be ashamed to love Him OUT LOUD!

Chapter 4:
Letting God Love Others Through Us

I'm in love with God- in Him I am complete. I'll give my life for Him. I lay it all down at His feet. I never want to love Him less. I never want to give Him second best. I'd rather lose it all than love Him less. He changed me in a moment. He filled my heart with his glory; He won my love. He takes my breath away.

1 John 4:19
"We love Him because He first loved us"

I talked about my experience with the love of God in my introduction. If you want, you can go back and read it again and remember your first experience with His great love. It's amazing when we experience His love for us - intellectually, emotionally and spiritually. It's more than a religious experience. I have known many who have had a religious or spiritual experience, but have not fully experienced God's love. To experience fully His love, we have to do so with body, soul and mind. Yes, it's hard to explain; it's immeasurable. Paul prayed for the Ephesians (Ephesians 3:17-19), "That Christ may dwell in your hearts through faith; that you, being rooted and grounded in love, may be able to comprehend with all the saints what is the width and length and depth and height — to know the love of Christ which passes knowledge; that you may be filled with all the fullness of God."

LOVE OUT LOUD

Sorry, but I have to say it. "Wow!" To know His love in 3D! His love is infinitely dimensional, and we can know this love more and more. But it passes knowledge; it has to be known and experienced personally in 3D. 1 John 3:1 says, "Behold what manner of love the father has bestowed on us, that we should be called children of God! (I love it when there is an exclamation mark in the Bible!) This is the greatness of His love for us, that He calls himself our Father and calls us His children. You cannot love your children more than God loves His children. I tell you what, I love my kids and my grandkids. As much as I love them- and would do anything for them- I don't think they could ever do anything to make me stop loving them, but God loves us more than all that!

Loving God is a reasonable reaction to experiencing His great love. If someone does not love God, I can only believe that they have never experienced (or are not experiencing) His great love. Our love for Him is our response to knowing how much He loves us.

Just recently, I saw a video about a backslidden youth pastor who was living under guilt, shame and condemnation to the point that he was living as a ragged street person. One day in an outdoor revival, God told a preacher to give his expensive ring to that ragged, smelly, dirty, street person. Not knowing who this beggar was, the preacher told him to come to the front. As he walked to the front, all the people began to stand up. The preacher could not know why the people reacted this way. He did not know that this man had been a prominent youth revivalist that ministered under a powerful anointing, and had been used of God to reach many young people. This youth minister had fallen prey to a witch who had set out to seduce him. When he finally fell with this woman, she told him that she had been sent to make him fall and that God would never forgive him. He had fallen into this life of despair and hopelessness, but now God was doing the unexpected to bring His beloved back to himself. When he got to the front, God confirmed His great love for him, and the young man was fully restored! Did this man ever stop loving God? I think he did, but it was because he could not experience the love of God. We can only love Him as a response to His love for us.

When we walk, or "exist" in His love, we then love God. Then, loving others is the natural by-product of that love. There is so much in the Bible about loving each other, especially in the book of 1 John. Take a look:

It starts in 1 John 2:5, "But whoever keeps His word, truly the love of God is perfected in him. By this we know we abide in Him."

Living God's word perfects our love; How's that for the importance of Bible study and Bible living? Jesus said in John 14 that if we abide in Him, and He abides in us, we will give much fruit. How do we know if we are abiding in Christ; Because we read the Bible and pray every day and/or we go to church three times a week? Yes, but even more than all that, it's because His love keeps on growing and showing in our lives.

1 John 2:10 NKJV
"He who loves his brother abides in the light, and there is no cause for stumbling in him."

There it is again, the word "love" and the word "abide" in the same verse. This time, it says that love keeps us in the light, and if we love, we don't cause our brothers to stumble or to be offended.

LOVE OUT LOUD

1 John 3:10
"In this the children of God and the children of the devil are manifest: Whoever does not practice righteousness is not of God, nor is he who does not love his brother."

There are children of God, and children of the devil. We are all God's creation, but that does not make us His children. We are not all the children of God. We are given that place when we receive our new nature at our re-birth. There are two things present in the children of God; first a life of practiced righteousness, and second; love toward our brothers in Christ.

1 John 3:14
"We know we have passed from death to life, because we love the brethren. He who does not love his brother abides in death."

Jesus said, "He that believes in me though he is dead he shall live." Love is the evidence that we have eternal life in us! Love demonstrates our faith - not miracles, healing, or great accomplishments. Love is what gives evidence of our faith.

1 John 3:16
"By this we know love, because He laid down His life for us, And we also ought to lay down our lives for the brethren."

The knowledge that God has loved me beyond all limits will compel me to go into the world to love others in the same way (my utmost for His highest).

How often do we have the opportunity to actually "lay down our lives" for one of our brothers in Christ? Here, God is saying that we should love each other with our lives; be willing to lay down our lives for each other. How can you know if you are able to lay down your life for one of your brothers? If we cannot lay down "our goods" for a brother in need, then we cannot even think that we would be willing to lay down our life for them. The next verse explains this.

1 John 3:17
"But whoever has this worlds goods, and sees his brother in need, and shuts up his heart from him, how does the love of God abide in him?"

The answer to the question? It does not. If we are not willing to lay down some money to help a brother who has a genuine need, then the love of God does not abide in us.

1 John 4:11
"Beloved if God so loved us, we also ought to love one another."

There are the familiar words "God so loved." I've heard those before. They're in John 3:16, "For God so loved the world that He gave His only begotten Son that whoever believes in Him will not perish but have everlasting life;" to love each other with the same love that God loved us. Sacrificial love; a love that gave His best; a love that "did not spare his own son but gave Him up freely for us."

"I believe He wants us to love others so much that we go to extremes to help them."
— Francis Chan, Crazy Love: Overwhelmed by a Relentless God

LOVE OUT LOUD

1 John 4:12
"No one has seen God at anytime. If we love one another God abides in us, and His love has been perfected in us."

Nobody can see God; He is the invisible God. So how does He make himself known? Like the wind, you cannot see it, but you can feel it! You cannot see it, but you can see the trees moving; you feel the effects of the wind. Love is the effect of God in our lives. Others see God through our love, feel God through our love; moved by the love of God that is in us and flows through us. God's love is perfected as we allow it to grow and show in our lives. People see God's love when we love out loud.

37 Ways to Love Each Other

1. **Be devoted to one another.**
   (Rom. 12:10)
2. **Give preference to one another.**
   (Rom. 12:10)
3. **Be of the same mind toward one another.**
   (Rom. 12:16)
4. **Accept one another by withholding judgment.**
   (Rom. 14:1)
5. **Accept one another by showing preference.**
   (Rom. 14:1–5; 15:7)
6. **Esteem [highly regard] one another in love.**
   (Rom. 14:5; Phil. 2:3).
7. **Build up one another.**
   (Rom. 14:19; 1 Thess. 5:11)
8. **Counsel one another.**
   (Rom. 15:14)
9. **Serve one another by showing deference in matters of liberty**
   (Gal. 5:13)

10. **Bear one another's sin burdens.**
    (Gal. 6:2)
11. **Be gentle with one another.**
    (Eph. 4:2)
12. **Be kind to one another so as to preserve unity.**
    (Eph. 4:32)
13. **Speak truth to one another.**
    (Eph. 4:25; Col 3:9)
14. **Submit to one another.**
    (Eph. 5:21).
15. **Show compassion to one another.**
    (Col. 3:12)
16. **Bear with the inherent sinfulness of one another.**
    (Col. 3:13)
17. **Forgive one another.**
    (Col. 3:13)
18. **Use Spirit-filled, Word-saturated music to teach and admonish one another.**
    (Col.3:16; Eph. 5:19)
19. **Comfort one another with the hope of Christ's return.**
    (1 Thess. 4:18)
20. **Encourage one another.**
    (1 Thess. 5:11)
21. **Live in peace with one another.**
    (1 Thess. 5:13)
22. **Seek good for one another.**
    (1 Thess. 5:15)
23. **Encourage one another to forsake unbelief and hardness of heart.**
    (Heb. 3:13)
24. **Stimulate one another to spiritual growth.**
    (Heb. 10:24)

25. **Encourage one another by faithful participation in your local church.**
    (Heb. 10:25).
26. **Confess sins to one another.**
    (James 5:16)
27. **Pray for one another's spiritual and physical healing**
    (James 5:16).
28. **Be long-suffering and patient toward one another.**
    (1 Peter 4:8; Eph. 4:2)
29. **Be hospitable to one another without complaint.**
    (1 Peter 4:9)
30. **Serve one another.**
    (1 Peter 4:10; Gal. 5:13)
31. **Act in humility toward one another.**
    (1 Peter 5:5)
32. **Show holy affection to one another.**
    (1 Peter 5:14)
33. **Participate in the holy walk with one another.**
    (1 John 1:7)
34. **Refuse to become resentful toward one another.**
    (1 John 3:11–12)
35. **Give sacrificially to meet one another's needs.**
    (1 John 3:16–17)
36. **Fight fear together by growing in love.**
    (1 John 4:18).
37. **Walk in truth together**
    (1 John 3:18; 2 John 1:5).

John 13:35
"By this all will know that you are My disciples, if you have love for one another."

LETTING GOD LOVE OTHERS THROUGH US

This verse is amazing! People will know that we follow Jesus, that we are the real thing, when they see us loving each other! Love will convince people. I believe that one of the key factors that will usher in a powerful revival and harvest of souls is when we, the people of God, begin to love God and one another as He commands.

> 1 John 4:17,18
> *"Love has been perfected among us in this: That we may have boldness in the Day of Judgment, because as He is, so are we in the world. There is no fear in love; but perfect love casts out fear, because fear involves torment. But he who fears has not been made perfect in love."*

Our love is perfected not in loving God, but in loving each other. There are so many believers who love God, but have a hard time loving others. God is easy to love! The real test of love is when we can love imperfect people; people who can be offensive, rude, arrogant, selfish, unreasonable, inconsiderate... should I go on? Yes, that's us; imperfect people! But love is perfected when we can love each other with a sincere, fervent and visible love. We will never walk as Jesus walked until we learn to love like Jesus loves. Then, we will have boldness before God. When we stand before God, we will not be thinking about whether or not we finished the building project, or how good those songs came out Sunday morning. We will not be concerned as to how many ministries we had in our church or how many crusades or conferences we held. We will not be thinking, "Maybe God is going to judge me because I didn't visit enough countries."

One of the things that will be foremost in our minds - and in God's mind, I believe - will be, "How did you treat your brothers? Did you show love to everyone?" If you have walked a life of "fervent love for the brethren", the Lord will be pleased

41

with you. If not, then you will be fearful when you stand before Him in judgment. I do not think that we will only be judged for how conflict-free we are able to live our life, but how fervently and affectionately were we able to love God's children. Were we willing to make sacrifices to help those in need, and to forgive and love- even those who offended us?

"What does love look like? It has the hands to help others. It has the feet to hasten to the poor and needy. It has eyes to see misery and want. It has the ears to hear the sighs and sorrows of men. That is what love looks like."
-- Saint Augustine

When we love out loud, others see our love; they cannot miss it. It's like being in a quiet room, and someone comes in shouting; everyone turns to see. That's what I want! I want to live my life so full of God's love that when others come close to me, they get God's love all over them. I want to "Love Out Loud!"

Chapter 5:
Loving God Through Our Worship

My heart cries out for you, I lift my hands to worship, I stand in awe of you; I want to see your face. You are my only strength, my trust is all in you. My light, my rock, my friend; You keep me from falling. My heart cries out, my spirit prays; stay close to me, and draw me closer to you. My heart cries out for you, Father I want you more. My heart cries out for you, Spirit I want you more. My heart cries out for you, Jesus I want you more, more than anything, more than anything.

When I worship Him, I feel complete, fulfilled and greatly loved. When I pour my love on Him - just letting it come from the deepest part of my heart, sometimes in a song, sometimes in prayer, sometimes in groaning, almost always with tears - there is nothing comparable. When I first came to Christ out of a life of darkness and drugs, after I had spent time worshiping Him, I would say that I had gotten an overdose of the Holy Ghost. But even that cannot describe what I experience every time that I enter that place of worship; where I pour out my heart to Him and He pours His great love upon me. One time as I was worshiping, God spoke to my heart and asked me, "Emilio, do you know what I like about you?" "No, God. I don't know what you like about me, what is it?" I replied. "What I like about you," He continued, "is that you are not ashamed to praise me, no matter where you are."

LOVE OUT LOUD

I love to praise Him; I love to worship Him in His presence. Worshipping God is just that, worshipping Him. *Worship* is defined as; "to show profound religious devotion and respect to; adore or venerate, to be devoted to and full of admiration for, to have or express feelings of profound adoration."

The most common word in the New Testament for *worship* is Proskuneo (προσκυνέω – pros-kü-ne'-ō). This word occurs sixty times in the New Testament; 57 of which are in the four gospels, Acts, and Revelation (the other three instances occur in 1 Corinthians 14, Hebrews 1, and Hebrews 11). It originally carried with it the idea of subjects falling down to kiss the ground before a king or to kiss their feet. The literal definition means "to kiss, like a dog licking his master's hand, to fawn or crouch to, homage (do reverence to, adore): worship."

Matthew 4:10 NIV
"Jesus said to him, 'Away from me, Satan! For it is written: Worship the Lord your God, and serve him only.'"

Here we learn that worship belongs only to God. Though other created beings may seek it, only God is deserving of our worship.

Matthew 8:2 NIV
"A man with leprosy came and knelt before him and said, 'Lord, if you are willing, you can make me clean.'"

Worship can be given because of a great need in our lives. Coming to God in faith in our time of need is pleasing to Him, and it honors Him.

Loving God Through Our Worship

Mark 5:6 NIV
"When he saw Jesus from a distance, he ran and fell on his knees in front of him."

As God draws near to us, we feel a natural draw to worship Him. His majesty and goodness causes us to run to Him and fall on our knees before Him.

Luke 24:50-53 NIV
"When he had led them out to the vicinity of Bethany, he lifted up his hands and blessed them. While he was blessing them, he left them and was taken up into heaven. Then they worshiped him and returned to Jerusalem with great joy. And they stayed continually at the temple, praising God."

This is pretty amazing. Jesus blessed His disciples, and then ascended into heaven. After He had ascended, they worshiped Him! This was the first time that Jesus received faith worship. No wonder Peter wrote what he did in 1 Peter 1:8.

1 Peter 1:8
"Whom having not seen you love. Though now you do not see Him, yet believing, you rejoice with joy inexpressible and full of glory."

Our faith is even greater as we worship by faith Him whom we have never seen with human eyes. What generates our worship? Love! Even though we have not seen Him we love Him- and oh how we love Him! Can you imagine His joy at our faith, as we passionately love the one we have only heard of? The one we have never seen but with our eyes of faith?

Look at what happened after they worshipped. Not the "returning to Jerusalem" part; the great joy part! Not just joy, but great joy. Later, the apostle Peter calls it "inexpressible joy". I like that the King James Bible calls it "Joy unspeakable and full of Glory", and the old song adds, "and the half has never yet been told". That's what happens every time we worship; our hearts are filled with and overwhelming, uncontainable, inexpressible, joy!

> John 4:23 NIV
> *"Yet a time is coming and has now come when the true worshipers will worship the Father in the Spirit and in truth, for they are the kind of worshipers the Father seeks."*

There was a point where my heart desired a position, and the Lord corrected me by asking me, "Emilio, what do you want to be?" He mentioned a few positions that I might have aspired. But almost immediately, the answer that God wanted came out of the depth of my heart and I answered; "I want to be a worshiper." There are many things that I want to do in life, but what I want to be in life is a worshiper. Truly, this is what God is seeking, true worshipers. What is true worship? First let's look at the truth of worship; God seeks worshipers that worship in truth.

Obedience, Sacrifice and Expression.

1. Obedience
Worship flows from your love of God as true worship (in spirit and in truth). "If you love me keep my commands." (John 14:15)

Do not get baptized or undertake your spiritual duties because you feel a religious or moral obligation; rather, because you love God and want to walk in obedience to Him.

LOVING GOD THROUGH OUR WORSHIP

2. Sacrifice

"Araunah gave it all to the king and said to him, 'May the Lord your God accept your offering.' But the king answered, 'No, I will pay you for it. I will not offer to the Lord my God sacrifices that have cost me nothing.' And he bought the threshing place and the oxen for fifty pieces of silver. Then he built an altar to the Lord and offered burnt offerings and fellowship offerings. The Lord answered his prayer, and the epidemic in Israel was stopped."
-- 2 Samuel 24:23-25 GNT

Worship should cost us, time, self and finances.

3. Expression

There is no unexpressed worship - whether it's kneeling, offering a sacrifice, lifting up hands or singing - worship is a verb. There are different ways to express, but we must never limit ourselves to one style or form of expression. We must express our love for Him in every way that we possibly can.

The Bible verse (John 4:23) says that God seeks worshipers who worship Him in Spirit. The spirit of our worship is that our worship, all of it; any of it, must come from our deep, passionate love for our Lord!

In Mark 10:21,22 we read; "Then Jesus looking at him, loved him, 'one thing you lack: Go your way, sell whatever you have and give to the poor, and you will have treasure in heaven; and come, take up the cross, and follow me.' But he was sad at this word, and went away sorrowful, for he had great possessions."

What does this have to do with worship? Please stay with me. The Lord was asking this young man to give up a fortune for a cross. The Bible says that he was sad because he had great possessions. What a contrast to those disciples who had given up everything. They returned to Jerusalem after having worshiped the Jesus they could not see, and they returned with great joy! You see, the verse says "Jesus loved this rich young ruler", but this man could not love him back. He would not worship Him.

Obedience: "Come, follow me."
Sacrifice: "Sell all that you have."
Expression: "Love me back, show me that you love me; follow me."

> Revelation 5:14 NIV
> *"The four living creatures said, "Amen," and the elders fell down and worshiped."*

Heaven is a place full of worship. Can you imagine expressing our love to Him for all eternity? Every time we set our eyes on Him, we will be drawn to worship. His abiding glory will constantly be drawing us into worship. Will God ever get tired of receiving all of this worship? Never! Revelation 4:11 says "You are worthy, O Lord, to receive glory and honor and power; for you created all things, and by your will they exist and were created." Colossians 1:16 says, "For by Him all things were created that are in heaven and that are on earth, visible and invisible, whether thrones or dominions or principalities or powers. All things were created through Him and for Him." Did you get that? All things were created for Him, all things were created to worship Him. God loves for us to worship Him out of a life of obedience and sacrifice. He wants us to worship Him with all of our heart, and with all of our love. This is why the first commandment is to "Love Him with all of our heart, soul and strength." I like what

Loving God Through Our Worship

David says in Psalms; "Bless the Lord, O my soul: and all that is within me, bless His holy name." All that is within me; all of my strength, all of my being, all my life, will bless Him.

Psalms 95:2 NKJV
"Let us come before His presence with thanksgiving; Let us shout joyfully to Him with Psalms."

Psalms 16:11 NKJV
"You will show me the path of life; In your presence is fullness of joy; At Your right hand are pleasures forevermore."

Not everyone who enters into His presence are true worshipers. Some are like the rich, young ruler who was sad because he could not offer true worship to Jesus. But all are called to be true worshippers; to make the sacrifices and to walk the road of obedience, to be willing to trade our fortune for a cross, to follow Him, and to love Him out loud.

Luke 7: 36-47
"Then one of the Pharisees asked Him to eat with him. And He went to the Pharisee's house, and sat down to eat. And behold, a woman in the city who was a sinner, when she knew that Jesus sat at the table in the Pharisee's house, brought an alabaster flask of fragrant oil, and stood at His feet behind Him weeping; and she began to wash His feet with her tears, and wiped them with the hair of her head; and she kissed His feet and anointed them with the fragrant oil. Then He turned to the woman and said to Simon, "Do you see this woman? I entered your house; you gave Me no water for My feet, but she has washed My feet with her tears and wiped them with the hair of her head. You gave Me no kiss, but this woman has not ceased to kiss My feet

49

since the time I came in. You did not anoint My head with oil, but this woman has anointed My feet with fragrant oil. Therefore I say to you, her sins, which are many, are forgiven, for she loved much. But to whom little is forgiven, the same loves little."

Worship flows from love. Where there is no love, there is no worship; where there is little love, there is little worship; where there is much love, there is much worship. Simon was not in love with Jesus- He had no worship to offer Him. This woman brought her perfume (of *great* value), and she made a great sacrifice. This woman came with tears of gratitude. You see, gratitude feeds love, but love is more than just gratitude. When ten lepers were healed, only one came back to give thanks and to worship (love) Jesus. The other nine had little or no gratitude; they had no love and no worship to offer. This woman made a sacrifice, came with tears, offered a service and worshiped because of the great love that she had for the Master.

I love it when my love for Christ becomes uncontainable! When my heart is filled with gratitude, I'm ready to lay everything down for my Lord if He asks it of me. I can worship Him with my whole heart, knowing that I am doing my all to live a life that is pleasing to Him- and endeavoring to do His perfect will.

Chapter 6:
The Greatest Chapter of All

There are many books written about faith, healings, miracles, success, victory; books that talk about how to win, how to excel, how to evangelize and disciple...etc. When is the last time you read a book about love? You do not hear too many sermons on love. It's as if preaching about love is old fashion; almost as if I preach about faith, it will portray me as a powerful man of God, but if I preach about love, it will make me look like a wimp. The Bible says that love is greater than hope, and even greater than faith! That means that Chapter 13 of 1 Corinthians is greater that Chapter 11 of Hebrews.

To learn how to love, we have to take a closer look at the greatest chapter of all; The Love Chapter.

I Corinthians 13:1
"Though I speak with the tongues of men and of angels, but have not love, I have become sounding brass or a clanging cymbal."

WITHOUT LOVE, THE GIFT OF TONGUES IS JUST NOISE!

LOVE OUT LOUD

Wait, I'm Pentecostal; I speak in tongues, and I love it. But love is more important than all of the gifts of the Spirit.

Without getting off the subject too much, just let me say that I believe that all the gifts of the Spirit are for all of us today. I have read a lot of books by those who believe different, and when they talk about the gifts, I usually skip that chapter, take it with some salt, or just cross it out. I have learned a lot from these non-charismatic teachers and preachers, but they cannot teach me what they have never experienced. I respect them, and respect their right not to be right about everything. The church of Corinth practiced praying in tongues and operating in the gift of tongues and interpretation- along with all the other gifts. When you pray or sing in tongues, you speak to God and edify your spirit (1 Corinthians 14:4). The Apostle Paul even went as far as to say that he spoke in tongues more than all of them and that he wished that everyone spoke with tongues (1 Corinthians 14:5,18). I said this to establish that speaking in tongues was considered at least by the Apostle Paul something very powerful and beneficial and yet if I have the gift of speaking in tongues and do not have love it will not do anyone any good.

Verse 2, *"And though I have the gift of prophecy, and understand all mysteries and all knowledge, and though I have all faith so that I could remove mountains, but have not love, I am nothing."*

WITHOUT LOVE I AM NOTHING

THE GREATEST CHAPTER OF ALL

Before we think that verse one was just a slam against speaking in tongues, take a good look at verse two. Prophecy (the gift to be most desired) and faith (probably the most desired gift operating in a life, and knowledge for all you professors and theologians) without love equal zero. If you want to be a zero in God's kingdom, just be loveless. In God's kingdom, it's how much you love, not how much you know or how good you look that makes you great.

Verse 3, *"And though I bestow all my goods to feed the poor, and though I give my body to be burned but have not love, it profits me nothing."*

This one can blow your mind. In today's "church world", with our focus on community service and social evangelism, it can be possible to help people and not love people. Will Mother Teresa "profit" eternally for all of her good works? I do not know; only God can determine that. If she (or anyone else who does good works in the name of Christ) truly loved God and was motivated by agape love, then it will be of profit. So can a person make great sacrifices, give everything they have to the poor, even give their lives, and not have love? Apparently so! All of our good deeds have to be motivated and driven by pure agape love; otherwise, we get nothing out of it.

"The hunger for love is much more difficult to remove than the hunger for bread."
- Mother Teresa

LOVE OUT LOUD

Verse 4, *"Love suffers long..."*

LOVE IS PATIENT

Many quit on their marriage, quit their job, quit on raising their kids and quit on life because they become impatient. If you love, you will have patience. If you want patience, you must have love; because patience comes from love. You can get patience from your trials or you can get patience from God's love. Just begin to love your husband, kids, boss, neighbor...etc, with the love of God, and you will have more than enough patience. Love with your thoughts, love with your words and love with your actions. I recently counseled a couple and told the wife to start showing loving behavior toward her husband (whom she resented). She listened to my advice - began to kiss him goodbye, call him sweetheart and be intentionally loving toward him - and God gave her a breakthrough that resulted in a revolutionized marriage.

Patience is a fruit of the Spirit; it will flow from a living relationship with the Lord. When we find ourselves being impatient, we need to ask ourselves if we have neglected our daily walk with the Savior; are we in love with God? Just because patience is of the fruit of the Spirit, does not mean that because we have received the Spirit, patience will automatically come to us. It's up to us to walk in the Spirit, and walking in the Spirit means walking in fellowship with the Lord. You do this by walking in obedience to His word, and by continual worship in your heart. Impatience in life and leadership is un-loving. When we are impatient with those that we lead or those around us, we fail to walk in love. Love those you lead through the patience that you show them. Allow them room for mistakes, remembering that your Master helps you when you make mistakes.

Verse 4 (continued), *"...Love is kind..."*

You cannot say that you love if you are rude. Rudeness is unacceptable. Some people are rude through sarcasm and some even display rudeness through humor. Rudeness can come in a lot of disguises, but if you belittle, devalue and offend people, you are rude. Love is kind.

Verse 4 (continued), *"...Love does not parade itself..."*

We like to do this. We like to stand out and be noticed. We like to look better than the other guy. We parade ourselves because it feels good to be the center of attention. When you grow in love, you do this a lot less. Love will pray, "Lord, let me decrease so that you can increase." You learn to shift attention to God or to someone else and reflect the glory elsewhere. If we do what we do to be seen and recognized by others, we are not doing it in love; we are parading ourselves.

Verse 4 (continued), *"...Is not puffed up..."*

There is nothing wrong with some godly pride when one of our kids wins a trophy or graduates from school. We all feel that. But being puffed up is being full of yourself. It's when people begin to tell you how great you preached or how great thou art and we begin to believe it. Praise, recognition and honor can go to our heads. Positions, gifts, talents and abilities can go to our head. Titles and degrees can go to our head. None of those things are bad; what is bad is when we get "puffed up" by them.

Verse 5, *"Love is not provoked"*

LOVE IS NOT EASILY ANGERED
Many get out of a marriage because they are angry all the time - an angry person is an unhappy person. You cannot be angry and happy at the same time. Many parents provoke their children

to anger by anger. If you get angry at your kids all the time, then you will raise angry kids. You have to have enough love to quit getting angry. Anger brings so many problems with it; abuse, violence, hate, pain, suffering, divorce...etc. I wonder how many who are reading this book have been affected by someone else's anger; I wonder how many are being affected by someone's anger right now? Or maybe, you are the angry person. Maybe you lose control, maybe you are angry all the time and you think it's normal. Anger is either a learned behavior in someone who existed in an atmosphere of anger, or an acquired behavior in someone who has become angry due to abuse, rejection or loss.

Proverbs 14:29 NKJV
"He who is slow to wrath has great understanding, But he who is impulsive exalts folly."

Why does it say that he that is slow to get angry has great understanding? There are things you must understand in order to keep from getting angry. You must understand yourself, know when you are getting angry and know how to keep anger from escalating. Anger comes at different levels; Annoyed, Irritated Frustrated, Upset, Mad/Angry, Rage, Out of Control. Most people do not let their anger go beyond frustrated or upset. Understand that if you are constantly getting angry, you have an anger problem.

You must understand how your anger is affecting those around you; it causes intimidation, fear, loss of peace, stress, and oppression. Anger creates a hostile environment. Your anger can quietly make others feel punished and afraid. You must understand that anger is never a solution. It may seem like it solves things, it may get you your desired result (or "payoff"), but then you are getting what you want through intimidation and manipulation. There is no relationship.

The Greatest Chapter of All

James 1:19-20 NKJV
"So then, my beloved brethren, let every man be swift to hear, slow to speak, slow to wrath; for the wrath of man does not produce the righteousness of God."

You must understand that apart from righteous anger, anger is not a good thing and not pleasing to God. Anger is sin from the sin nature.

Gal. 5:19-21 NKJV
*"Now the works of the flesh are evident, which are: adultery, fornication, uncleanness, lewdness, idolatry, sorcery, hatred, contentions, jealousies, **outbursts of wrath**, selfish ambitions, dissensions, heresies, envy, murders, drunkenness, revelries, and the like; of which I tell you beforehand, just as I also told you in time past, that those who practice such things will not inherit the kingdom of God."*

Did you see it? I put it in bold letters for you, "outbursts of wrath." Sound familiar? Anger is related to foolishness.

Ecclesiastes 7:9 NKJV
"Do not hasten in your spirit to be angry, for anger rests in the bosom of fools."

Anger is associated with grieving the Holy Spirit.

Ephesians 4:30-31 NKJV
"And do not grieve the Holy Spirit of God, by whom you were sealed for the day of redemption. Let all bitterness, wrath, anger, clamor, and evil speaking be put away from you, with all malice."

Anger is always accompanied by other sins.

Proverbs 29:22 NKJV
"An angry man stirs up strife, and a furious man abounds in transgression."

Proverbs 16:32 NKJV
"He who is slow to anger is better than the mighty, and he who rules his spirit than he who takes a city."

God wants you to have victory over your anger. It's not as if we can never get angry, but we must come to a place where we are slow to anger so that it takes a lot to make you angry, and even when you get angry, you "rule your own spirit". Anger does not control you; you control the anger. A lady once came to Billy Sunday and tried to rationalize her angry outbursts. "There's nothing wrong with losing my temper," she said. "I blow up, and then it's all over." "So does a shotgun," Sunday replied, "and look at the damage it leaves behind!"

"It is he who is in the wrong who first gets angry..."
- William Penn

I offer you these four things to help you overcome your anger:

1. Think before you speak or act.

2. Never give yourself permission to get angry.

3. Always confess your anger as sin to God and to the person your anger was directed towards. Ask for forgiveness and ask that person to pray for you.

4. Go back and deal with all unresolved anger. Forgive.

You do not need anger management; you need love. Anger management can help you deal with your rage when you feel it, but love will cause you to quit being an angry person. Consider that your anger problem is really a love problem; whom do you get angry at all the time? Ask God to flood you with love for that person. Have you lost your love for your wife, husband, children? It can happen - we go through so much in life. You want to love each other, but you've hurt each other so much. Love covers a multitude of sin. If you are angry at someone all the time, you are not loving that person.

Verse 5 (continued), "...*love thinks no evil...*"
(CJB version says, "keeps no record of wrong".)

Cancel the debt; throw away the records of the past. Quit playing them over and over; take them off your play list. Quit trying to collect for past damages every time you have a problem. Jesus never brings up your past. Some say, "I can't forgive," but the truth is that you will not forgive. Some say, "It's too hard," or "too painful." Jesus understands; He will help you with the pain. There has to be a once-and-for-all; you will not continue. You cannot love if you do not forgive.

Verse 6, "Love does not rejoice in iniquity but rejoices in truth."

Love cares about the right and wrong. It's not just a mushy feeling, but the driving force that pushes us to seek after righteousness- to speak out for truth and justice. When the love of God is in you, you hate what God hates and love what God loves.

LOVE OUT LOUD

Our involvement as children of God in righting the wrongs of this world is more than a social responsibility, it's responsible love.

Verse 7, *"Love bears all things, Believes all things, hopes all things, endures all things."*

Perfect strength, perfect faith and perfect hope are only found in perfect love. We will never love perfectly in this life. We can only grow in love and abound in love more and more. A perfect love in us is a healthy, growing, vibrant love. Jesus walked in this perfect love. Early in my Christian life, I was presented with the challenge of replacing the name of Jesus with the word "love" in these verses. It flowed so naturally and perfectly. Jesus is patient and kind. Jesus bears all things, believes all things, hopes all things, endures all things. Then I was to try it again using my name in place of the word "love". Emilio is patient. I did not get very far before I realized that it did not flow very well at all. When it comes to love, we all have a long way to go.

Verse 8, *"Love never fails."*

I wish I could love like that. I wish that my love for God was so strong that I could (because of my great love for Him) overcome every temptation, walk every minute in the Spirit, love others the way He did, and the way He does. Thank God that His love never fails! He will never stop loving me. His love will take me to the very end and give me a place at His side - in His kingdom - forever!

Love always protects, trusts, hopes and perseveres. There is consistency in love. Jesus is the same yesterday, today and forever. We should be like Him. You cannot be loving one day and hateful the next. You cannot be kind one week and rude the next. You cannot be a Christian for one month and live without Christ the next month. The Bible says that a double-minded man is unstable in all his ways (James 1:8). Unstable people do not remain. Unstable people do not stay in one relationship. They are undependable; they bring insecurity to the family.

Keep doing the right thing; do not grow weary in well doing, do not get tired of loving. It takes work to love. Love is never unfaithful, never defrauding, adulterating, or cheating. I tell young people to start developing a faithful spirit - that when you find the right person, you get married in your spirit first. That means that you feel married to that person (does not mean you are married). You begin to act as though you are married to that person (not physically) in your faithfulness and loyalty. Become marriage material. For those of us who are married, the greatest test of our love will be how we love our spouse. We have to take all of the scriptures that talk about loving others and apply them to our relationship with our spouse. If it's not there, it's not anywhere.

The first thing you can do to love your fiancé is to make a lifelong commitment in marriage. Contrary to the famous hit song sang by Paul Anka released in 1974, *You're Having My Baby,* the song starts out with the words "Having my baby, what a lovely way to say I love you..."

It's a ring (a lifelong commitment), not a baby that gives witness to a genuine godly love. Babies are always a blessing and as Rick Warren said in his book *The Purpose Driven Life,* "There are no illegitimate children, only illegitimate parents." Marriage, as defined by the Bible, was instituted by God so that a man and a woman could consummate their love under divine approval. Children are to be born in the bonds of holy wedlock, and be raised to know and fear the Lord under a loving relationship.

LOVE OUT LOUD

To truly love your spouse, you must nurture her/him. Love is nurturing, and nurturing takes time and devotion. Love is like a garden; it requires constant maintenance. A loving relationship requires work, intentionality, taking out the weeds and making sure it gets enough water. To have a loving relationship, we have to be willing to invest plenty of time into it. How can you say you love God, whom you cannot see, if you cannot love your husband or wife that you see every day?

Learn to be faithful to God and faithful in the little things. Learn to be faithful to your responsibilities and in the relationships you already have with family and friends. Then when you are in the marriage relationship, you will not have a problem with unfaithfulness.

Verse 11, *"Love puts away childish things. Love goes on to maturity."*

Children never stay at anything very long. They move from one thing to another- short attention span. Some people are just immature; they go from one relationship to another, from one job to another, or from one house to another. How many remember when you were like that; Immature, and everyone around you suffers for it? You do not have to throw temper tantrums when you do not get your way; grow up. Love will bring you into maturity- emotionally and spiritually. Failure to grow is due to lack of love. If you love God, you will put away childish things- those unloving, selfish words, attitudes and actions that are due to immaturity. Remaining immature is a lack of love for God, and lack of love for those around you. This is why we must continue to grow in love by allowing the Holy Spirit to teach us.

THE GREATEST CHAPTER OF ALL

John 15:4-7

"Abide in Me, and I in you. As the branch cannot bear fruit of itself, unless it abides in the vine, neither can you, unless you abide in Me." "I am the vine, you are the branches. He who abides in Me, and I in him, bears much fruit; for without Me you can do nothing. If anyone does not abide in Me, he is cast out as a branch and is withered; and they gather them and throw them into the fire, and they are burned. If you abide in Me, and My words abide in you, you will ask what you desire, and it shall be done for you."

1 John 4:16

"Who ever lives (remains) in love lives (remains) in God."

The power of love is the power to remain. Living in love is the power to remain. You can have faith, but if you do not have love, it will not work. You can have hope, but without love, it will not last. You need love to remain, to endure, to persevere, and to see things through. It's love that will keep you going; where all else fails, love never fails.

Galatians 5:22 talks to us about the fruit of the Spirit... ***But the fruit of the Spirit is:***

Love, [it all begins with love. If there is not a passionate love in your heart, you will not have any of the others mentioned here.]

Joy, [have you ever had to be under a supervisor or a boss that had no joy? I'm sure we have all had this experience at one time or another. To work under a leader that has no joy is a

miserable job but what a difference when you work under someone joyful. Are you a joy to work with? To work for?]
Peace... [in the day and age we live in your workers need to find peace. As their leader you will radiate what is in your heart.]

The Bible teaches us how to live free from unhealthy stress and anxiety. We are to cast all of our cares upon Him; we are commanded to be anxious in nothing, but to make our request known to God with thanksgiving. Stress will block the flow of love in your life, and can even make you unloving. If we truly live the life of faith, we will walk in perfect peace. Peace comes from a courageous disposition of trust in God's love and care for us in all of our times of need and tribulation. You will not be an effective leader if you are leading out of fear; you must lead with peaceful courage. Like Joshua, God commanded him to be strong and of good courage! God commanded Joshua not to fear! He had to find peace in his heart to successfully lead God's people into the battles that were ahead. Many times, Jesus told his followers, "Fear not" and "Peace". He not only told them, but he demonstrated peace in every situation. When the storm was rocking the boat and the disciples were full of fear, Jesus was resting! Even when He was confronted with the pain and suffering that he was to undergo, He found peace at the garden of Gethsemane.

> *"Darkness cannot drive out darkness; only light can do that. Hate cannot drive out hate; only love can do that."*
> - Martin Luther King, Jr.

Galatians 5:22-23
"But the fruit of the Spirit is love, joy, peace, long-suffering, kindness, goodness, faithfulness, gentleness, self-control."

THE GREATEST CHAPTER OF ALL

If we are to become good leaders, we must first become good lovers- lovers of God and lovers of others. We must grow in love until His love perpetuates and radiates in us, and through us, until we are patient, loving, kind, faithful and gentle. Only after we learn to love can we learn to be the leaders that God intended for us to be.

Chapter 7:
Leading With Love

My first book *Leading With Vision* was all about preparing for, understanding and fulfilling your God-given vision. I believe that vision is very vital to leadership, but vision without love is mechanical, self-serving and humanistic. Just because you can be a CEO in a large company does not mean you can be a "good shepherd". To be a good leader, you have to lead with love.

You will never be a good leader if you do not love the people you lead. You could become a great leader, but you will never be a "good" leader. Jesus said that he is the "good" shepherd not the "great" shepherd. The Greek word *kalos,* translated "good", describes that which is noble, wholesome, good, and beautiful; in contrast with that which is wicked, mean, foul and unlovely. It signifies not only that which is good inwardly—character—but also that which is attractive outwardly. It is an innate goodness. Therefore, in using the phrase "the good shepherd", Jesus is referencing His inherent goodness, His righteousness, and His beauty. As the shepherd of the sheep, He is the one who protects, guides, and nurtures His flock.

To be *good* is to be humble, to have integrity; to lead with love. Moses loved the people; he was willing to do anything or make any sacrifice for them. Solomon could have asked for anything, and yet he asked for wisdom to lead God's people. He wanted the best for them because he loved them. Jesus was the "Good Shepherd". The good shepherd lays down his life for the sheep. To be a great shepherd in the eyes of God, we first have to be good shepherds. Jesus said in Matthew 20:26, "Yet it shall not be so among you; but whoever desires to become great among you, let him be your servant." We have to be willing to make sacrifices for the flock. This includes, many times, sacrificing our egos, our pride and our agendas. I'm learning that it's about the people, not about the project.

I knew a pastor who was always criticizing and labeling his congregation. His words were to the effect of; "these people are ruined or rotten to the core." Over a period of about three months, I would hear him make such comments. Finally, one day, when he spoke out his harsh words against the people that he was called to shepherd, I could not hold back any longer. This had bothered me from the first time that it would happen. I would try to encourage him, but this time, before I could stop myself, out came the rebuke. "If you can't love these people, then you should not be their pastor. Find something else to do because these people need someone who will love them unconditionally!" He was almost as stunned at hearing these words as I was that I had spoken them.

Before D.L. Moody became the greatest evangelist of the 19th Century, he ran a storefront Sunday School to reach some of the street kids of Chicago. The story is told of one tough little guy who was seen Sunday after Sunday, trudging by on his way to that Sunday School. He lived a long way from his destination. On one brutally cold and snowy day, one man saw the boy walking into the wind, stubbornly making his usual Sunday morning journey to Moody's Sunday School. He asked the boy why he would make that effort every Sunday, even on a day when no one else was out- especially when he passed many churches that were much closer to his home.

LEADING WITH LOVE

The boy's explanation was clear and simple: "I go there because they sure make a fellow feel loved there."

Honestly, it's not always easy to be a good shepherd. I have to admit, there have been times in my ministry when I responded in a unloving way or treated someone with a lack of love. It's not easy to love everyone all the time. I've had to learn things like how to hate a behavior without hating the person, and how to look at the person that is hardest to love with compassion. Loving God's sheep, all of them, must be the goal of every Christian leader, and also loving those that have not yet come to Christ.

Jesus asked Peter three times, "Do you love me Peter?" When Peter would say "yes", Jesus would immediately give the command "Feed my sheep." What is the connection between loving Jesus and feeding His sheep? Everything! You see, Jesus was not going to be there to be the object of Peter's manifested love, but that which Jesus loved the most, that which Jesus longed to care for personally but would not be able to; needed to be loved. His sheep; His precious sheep.

How do we love His precious sheep; these sheep that, at times, can be so stubborn? These sheep that tend to wander and get into so many problems and make so many mistakes? The thought of how Jesus takes one of the sheep, gives him a staff and a rod and then tells that sheep, "Okay, now go out there and act like a shepherd" is mind boggling to me. What a great act on behalf of the Chief shepherd to give to a mere sheep the position of shepherd. Oh, how we need to have the Great Shepherd's heart and hear his voice so that He can shepherd the sheep through us. His command to us shepherds is the same as it was to Peter, "Feed my sheep!" I believe He is saying, "My sheep will have many needs; meet their needs!" I do not believe that this just means preach to them every Sunday, even though I'm sure this is a great part of feeding the sheep. I think it is a responsibility to us shepherds to make sure that the people in our care are being cared for. One of the greatest models for pastoral leadership is one that I found in the Psalms 23:

Psalm 23:1 AMP
"THE LORD is my Shepherd [to feed, guide, and shield me], I shall not lack."

The Lord is my shepherd... "Jehovah Roi"

He is the good Shepherd; our greatest example as we lead His sheep. As you study the life of Jesus, you see the great example that He has given us. He has shown us how to love the sheep by living his life for (and even laying his life down) for the sheep. We have to have the heart of the Chief Shepherd. We have to abide in Him. We have to walk close to Him, so that He can shepherd His sheep through us.

I shall not lack... "Jehovah Jireh"

We are to be providers to those we lead. We must be able to discern the needs of those we are leading through prayer, by listening to them and having compassion. We are called to meet physical, emotional, and most of all, spiritual needs in the flock.

Psalm 23:2 AMP
"He makes me lie down in [fresh, tender] green pastures; He leads me beside the still and restful waters."

Judges 6:24
The Lord our peace..."Jehovah Shalom"

LEADING WITH LOVE

It is our work to make sure that the sheep eat and drink. Sheep, by nature, are high strung, nervous and easily stressed. It is only when they feel safe and secure (and after they have eaten), that they will lay down and rest. As loving leaders, we, through the word and our love, can bring safety and security to the hearts of those we are called to feed. Sheep will not drink from moving water. It is up to us to create a peaceful atmosphere for those we lead. We must labor to keep a conflict-free environment, endeavoring to keep the unity of the spirit in the bonds of peace (Ephesians 4:3), I have seen this, and I am still learning. It has been a hard lesson for me. I have a very trusting nature and tend to avoid conflict. I am a peacemaker by nature. There have been times that I should have been harder on those who caused strife and division in the congregation. I have let things go by and limited my action to "praying about it". I have seen people bring division, and I have seen how much the "flock" is affected by it. I am committed to taking a much stronger stand against strife for the sake of the lambs.

The righteous God: "El Tisaddik"

Psalm 23:3 AMP
"He refreshes and restores my life (my self); He leads me in the paths of righteousness [uprightness and right standing with Him--not for my earning it, but] for His name's sake."

If we love the Shepherd, we will love His sheep. If we love His sheep, we will refresh and restore their lives. His sheep live in a hostile world. The world hates them! Many times, they have to suffer persecution and scorn. Even in America, most people are not Christian-friendly, and many of them (even though they try to be polite and civil), the moment one of His sheep stands up for truth and righteousness, they are "taken to the slaughter". It's not easy being one of His sheep. The sheep need a loving shepherd that will refresh them through His words. This does not mean that we do not correct and rebuke the sheep. There are times when the shepherd had to correct the sheep for their own spiritual good, but what the sheep need most is refreshing and restoration. Jesus did not say, "If you love me, beat my sheep". He said, "Feed my sheep". Never do we demonstrate greater love for the Master than when we are laboring with love and taking care of His sheep.

The all-sufficient God: "El Shaddai"

> Psalm 23:4 AMP
> *"Yes, though I walk through the [deep, sunless] valley of the shadow of death, I will fear or dread no evil, for You are with me; Your rod [to protect] and Your staff [to guide], they comfort me."*

We must remember that people go through very hard places and difficult seasons in life. His sheep suffer in their physical bodies, in their relationships and their finances. Many times, they struggle with personal issues such as guilt, anger, shame and poor self-image. God's sheep suffer many losses, failures and setbacks. Sometimes they go through deep, dark valleys. Life can be so complex We can be so complex. His sheep need to know that we are with them; they need to know that God is with them. We must comfort God's people. For this, we must help them to see the all-sufficient God. We must model to them and teach them that God is more than enough. God's children need a lot of encouragement, inspiration and most of all, love.

LEADING WITH LOVE

The mighty God: "El Gibbor"

Psalm 23:5 AMP
"You prepare a table before me in the presence of my enemies. You anoint my head with oil; my [brimming] cup runs over."

As loving shepherds, we too must be willing and able to do spiritual warfare for those under our care. When they are in the house of God, they must be able to rest and feast no matter what battles they have in their lives. They must find a table prepared for them in the house of God. It is up to us to make "church" a place of feasting, rejoicing and a place where the presence of the Holy Spirit is overflowing. As shepherds, it's up to us to make sure that God's people are led into God's presence. I believe that every time we come together, we give time for God's manifested Spirit to move in people's hearts. I believe that worship time in the church is not just a time to sing some fast and some slow songs and experience a taste of His glory. I believe that "worship time" (that time that we dedicate to focus just on Him and to sing to him), this is the "love feast" mentioned in Jude 1:12. This is when we pour out our love to God in worship, and where God pours out His love on us by the Holy Spirit.

The Holy God: "El Hakkadosh"

Psalms 23:6
"Surely goodness and mercy shall follow me all the days of my life; And I will dwell in the house of the Lord forever."

God's people have been "set apart" for Him. They are HIS sheep, not ours. We are mere stewards of His sheep. His sheep are destined for a life of goodness and mercy. We are separated to be holy unto the Lord, to dwell in His presence forever. It is a great honor to be called to be a shepherd and work together with the "good and greatest Shepherd". Being in church leadership is, in my opinion, one of the greatest privileges that we can have. It's also one of the greatest, if not THE greatest, responsibility anyone can ever have. So many people take it so lightly to be in leadership. Not me; I feel so honored to be a pastor. I felt honored to be a youth leader and a Sunday school teacher. I have always felt that these are God-given responsibilities He has entrusted me with. I have always felt that I will give an account to Him for my faithfulness and my love for those He entrusts to me.

1 Peter 5:1 NKJV
"The elders who are among you I exhort, I who am a fellow elder and a witness of the sufferings of Christ, and also a partaker of the glory that will be revealed..."

As a "fellow elder", I want to tell you that being called to be a pastor is a great privilege and a great joy. In the ministry, there are "seasons" of great joy and seasons of hardship. By the time this book is published, I will have been a full-time lead pastor for 29 years; I have pretty much seen it all and lived it all. My experience has been a great one! Most of my 29 years have been filled with excitement, vision, harvest and "goodness and mercy". However, I must say that those days of hardship, sacrifice, betrayal and loss can seem like years. I would not trade any of it; not the good and not the, well, "difficult" times. I have learned, grown and become a better person through it all.

Verse 2, *"Shepherd the flock of God, which is among you, serving as overseers, not by compulsion but willingly, not for dishonest gain but eagerly..."*

LEADING WITH LOVE

Here are our orders; "Shepherd my sheep (His flock) ...serving..." The task of feeding the sheep is a task of serving. This will require a servant's heart. If you do not have a servant's heart, you will not faithfully fulfill your calling. Our service must come from a heart that is eager to serve our Lord. If we do this because we feel that we "have to" do it, we will not be serving from the heart. If we "serve" to see how much we can get out of it for ourselves, we will not be good shepherds. If we serve out of carnal motives, we will damage the sheep and suffer the correction of the Shepherd. We must have a willingness that comes from knowing that we have been chosen by the Shepherd. Our work must be done eagerly and wholeheartedly. Ephesians 6:7-8 says that we should do the will of God from the heart, "with goodwill doing service as to the Lord and not to men, knowing that whatever good anyone does, he will receive the same from the Lord...." We work and labor for the sheep, and for the reward that the Chief Shepherd will give us one day.

Verse 3, "...nor as being lords over those entrusted to you, but being examples to the flock..."

We are not called to be taskmasters, but overseers. We are called to lead by example. The state of the flock comes before "progress"! A lot of us as pastors/leaders are very result driven. I do not think that is always a bad thing, until we lose sight of God's priorities. People are always first, and our priority has to be to give them with an example they can follow; not just an example of holiness and works, but of tender love and compassion. Remember I said that God has a way of making me feel like I'm the only one that He loves with all of His heart? I wonder if I can make others feel that way...

Verse 4, *"...and when the Chief Shepherd appears, you will receive the crown of glory that does not fade away."*

Here is the best part. We are called to be under-shepherds with the Chief Shepherd! We are called to work together with Christ. When He comes, we will receive a special reward for our faithful service to His sheep.

I am far from being comparable to the Chief Shepherd, but I am trying my best and I believe I am improving every day.

Conclusion

As I bring this book to an end, I am so thankful for the love God has shown me, and for the love He has put in my heart. I want to love Him more, and I want to love others more. Loving God and loving others is the heart of all we are and all we do as children of God. At the end of your days, all that will last, all that will be rewarded in eternity, are the things you did out of love. I want to love God more; I want to love my wife and my family more, I want to love God's people more; I want to love the world of lost people, more. I am not content with my love life; I want my love to abound. As I write this, I am finishing twenty-eight years of ministry; fourteen years as the Lead pastor of Centro Cristiano del Valle in Manson Washington and fourteen years as Lead pastor of New Life Covenant Church in Avondale Arizona. God has been good to me- much, much more that I deserve. I was destined for ruin, failure and destruction. God saved me and made something beautiful out of my life. Recently, the Lord showed me that I was in my third season of ministry. 14 years in Washington, 14 years in Arizona and now my third season of 14 years. At the end of this next season, I will be 70 years old. I know, I can't believe it either. I was just eighteen years old when I met Jesus. Man, did I fall in love with Him! Now, we have walked together for almost 39 years. He has been so good to me. I love Him so much more; I have so much more to love Him for. He not only rescued me and transformed me, but He exalted me and blessed me with earthly and spiritual blessings. Even though I came from a broken home, He gave me a godly wife, children and grandchildren that fear the Lord. Even though I lacked the proper education, He has used me in high-leadership positions within my denomination and within the Kingdom of God. He has been and is, my provider, my protector, my advocate, and my guide. He is everything to me. I never want to love Him less. I never want not to be in love with Him. He has enlarged my territory, given me the promised land, allowed me to lead slaves out of Egypt and equip the saints for the work of the ministry. I wish I could better describe the greatness of His love. So as I search for my final words, I find these:

THANK YOU God for loving me. Thank you GOD for loving me, Thank you God for loving ME. Thank you God for LOVING me! Over and again, your love for me astounds me. Thank you Jesus for being my savior and my friend; thank you for loving me. You are my past, my present and my future. If I could ask for only one thing, it would be that my love for my Savior would increase, more and more.